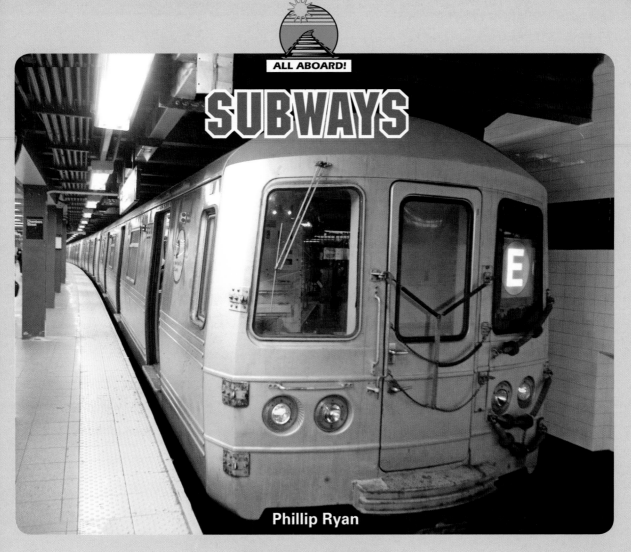

SUBWAYS

ALL ABOARD!

Phillip Ryan

PowerKiDS
press™

New York

Published in 2011 by The Rosen Publishing Group, Inc.
29 East 21st Street, New York, NY 10010

First Edition

Editor: Joanne Randolph
Book Design: Ashley Burrell
Photo Researcher: Jessica Gerweck

Photo Credits: Cover © Sylvain Grandadam/age fotostock; pp. 5, 6–7, 10–11, 14–15, 18–19, 21, 24 (bridge, platform, seats) Shutterstock.com; p. 9 © Factoria Singular/age fotostock; p. 13 Brian Summers/Getty Images; p. 17 © Dennis MacDonald/age fotostock; p. 22 © www.iStockphoto.com/Denis Tangney Jr.; p. 24 (station) Jean Heguy/age fotostock.

Library of Congress Cataloging-in-Publication Data
Ryan, Phillip.
  Subways / by Phillip Ryan. — 1st ed.
      p. cm. — (All aboard!)
  Includes index.
  ISBN 978-1-4488-0636-2 (library binding) — ISBN 978-1-4488-1213-4 (pbk.) —
ISBN 978-1-4488-1214-1 (6-pack)
  1. Subways—Juvenile literature. I. Title.
TF845.R936 2011
  388.4'28—dc22
                              2009049317

Manufactured in the United States of America

CPSIA Compliance Information: Batch #WS10PK: For Further Information contact Rosen Publishing, New York, New York at 1-800-237-9932

CONTENTS

Have you ever seen a subway train? One is waiting at the **platform** now!

5

Lots of people ride subway trains. Subways carry them where they need to go.

You need to pay to get into the subway **station**. Sometimes people use a card to pay.

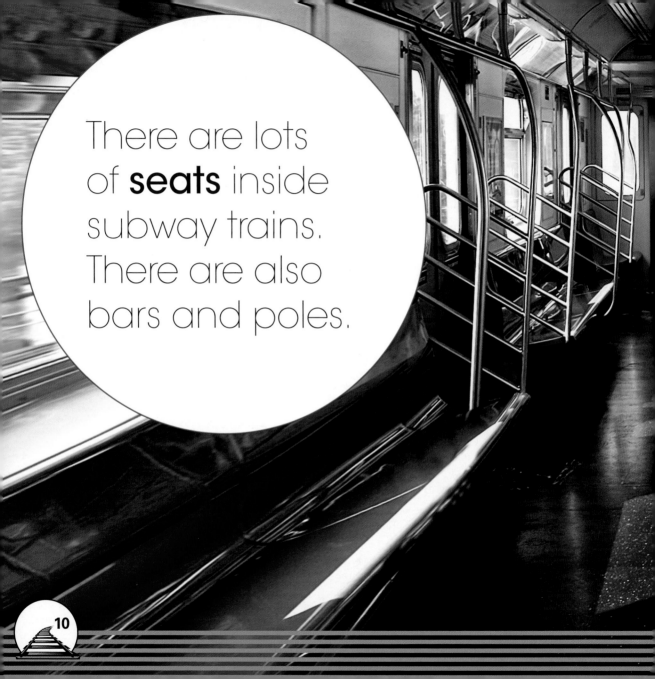

There are lots of **seats** inside subway trains. There are also bars and poles.

Some people sit on the seats. Others stand and hold on to the bars and poles.

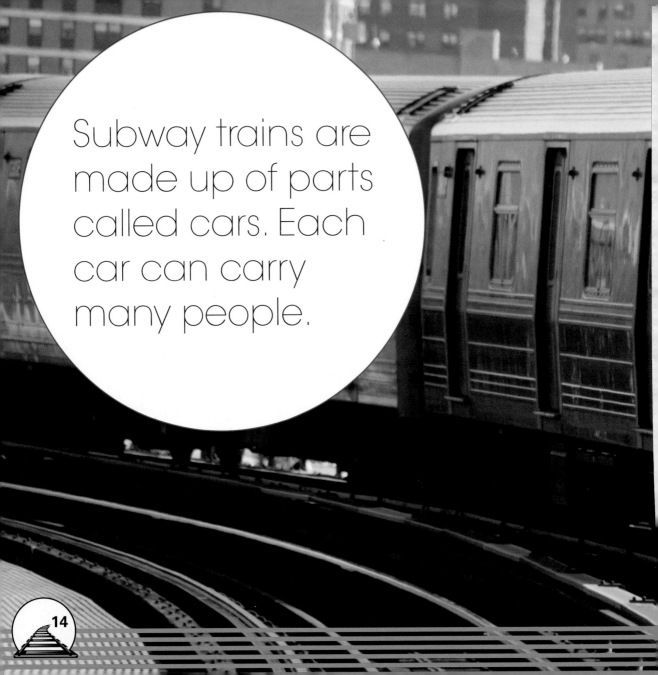

Subway trains are made up of parts called cars. Each car can carry many people.

Subway stations have maps. These maps help you find out which train goes to your stop.

Most subway stations are underground. Many of the tracks are underground, too.

ПУТЬ 3 ПУТЬ 4

19

Sometimes subway tracks are above ground. This subway goes over a **bridge**.

Are you ready to take a ride on the subway?

WORDS TO KNOW

bridge

 platform

seats

 station

WEB SITES

Due to the changing nature of Interne links, PowerKids Press has developed an online list of Web sites related to the subject of this book. This site is updated regularly. Please use this link to access the list:
www.powerkidslinks.com/allabrd/sub